RAYMOND GRANT

authorHOUSE

AuthorHouse™
1663 Liberty Drive
Bloomington, IN 47403
www.authorhouse.com
Phone: 1 (800) 839-8640

Edited by Jeanne Marie Leach

All Bible Scriptures are taken from King James Version of the Bible.

Published by AuthorHouse 07/19/2017

ISBN: 978-1-5462-0052-9 (sc)
ISBN: 978-1-5462-0051-2 (e)

Library of Congress Control Number: 2017911266

Print information available on the last page.

This book is printed on acid-free paper.

Section 1

KINGDOM COME

A Pictureless Sky

Imagine a pictureless sky.
Why?
What is said will be—
When the time comes,
If you're aware of the time to come,
What is seen will be undone by the undoing of man
For sinful deeds in following the initiator of sin—the devil.
Picture no light
Or the light of day falling away
Never to return.
Is this a perfect picture?
Is this one which pleases the eye
Or brings comfort to the heart?
Surely not.
But surely these things and more will come to pass
Before that great and terrible day—
A day of joy and terror,
Hope and despair,
Fate and judgment.
A day like no other
Or ever shall be.
Rewards for the faithful,
But the guilty will be judged, to their despair.

An Hour to Come

An hour to come
Where there is no room for fun.
Instead, the desperate cries to save one's soul.
How many would dare come if they had known their outcome?
Will you cry to them with passion and mercy?
Call to them
That they might be saved from the hour to come,
Which no one knows?
Yet, it stands sure,
And surely the end is not calm.

Appropriating Favor

Appropriating the favor of God is by way of the heart.
A heart for God is a pull on his favor.
He pleases the ones who pleases Him.
His desires exceed ours;
He wants more for us than we want for ourselves.
Appropriate His favor;
Appropriate His grace.
By His grace, believers are saved.
Our salvation is nothing we accomplish in our own strength.
Instead, it's what God does for us.
How can we appropriate what He so freely gives?
It's when we look to please Him with our whole heart
He will hold back nothing.
Instead,
Gives us all.

Chipper Tink

Chipper tink---
What a word . . .
Or is it a word?
Not to be heard
Is a voice of silent thunder.
Can there be a movement without noise?
If a noise is not heard, will anything be heard?
I have not given My people a voiceless message
Yet many remain silent
As if their salvation is created for silent existence.
The Word, My Word must be heard.
A stifled tongue does no good to Me or for the kingdom.
My people must speak,
For it is I who will speak through them.
A militant host will rise up.
Who, in turn, will stand up for the kingdom of God?
For Me?
Silence hides one's faith.
Not flamboyance or with prideful exuberance,
But speak.
Even if with a soft voice
Speak,
For I have called you to this.
My people must speak
Otherwise, My Word will not spread to a dying breed
If you are saved,
Breathe life through the spoken Word
So others can experience the same value of life

Close Up

I am close to a willing and an obedient heart;
I am close in the life of the faithful.
My presence is known where they know Me,
Fear Me,
Revere Me.
I am close to faithful people with faithful deeds.
If you ever wondered about My presence,
Consider, if you will,
If I have ever fulfilled a need.

Ways undetectable.
Knowledge undeniable.
Arms outstretched.
So My people will benefit for My glory.

Crazed

Crazy and waiting,
Waiting and hoping,
Hoping without watching,
Though pursuing with all will.
Let not the worry of this life trouble you,
For every season has its due—
Due time, due punishment, due reward.
A reward is worth waiting for, despite the trials of life.
One perseveres for the point of faith,
And faith must be all-in-all
The end all
If one hopes to receive the prize

Deception in the Manor

Deception abounds in the manor
In the house—
The house of God as we know it today.
Many people are not fully engaged.
Instead, many are at work trying to drive the saved away.
Theirs is but a lost cause,
For I keep mine—
Those who are fully mine.
Still the deception exists.
The ungodly persist.
But in time
The deeds of deception will be brought to light.

Décor

Decoration.
The flavor of the month.
One drawing many
While others refusing to come.
Come by this way.
"Come by this way," it calls.
But who will answer the call?
Words not spoken, but a message is sent
Saying, "Come inside,"
Assuming there is where the work truly begins.
We are not of that sort
Drawing in because of decorations.
Instead, we live the truth in righteousness.
It is His light that draws,
His Word that compels.
Even our personal testimonies draw some near.
Not by the outward dress,
Rather the garment worn upon the heart—
One clothed in righteousness.
Far from the spectator's glance
Is a chance
To draw some in.
Far from the outward look
The message is spoken within.
The peace of God.
The mercy of God.
The love of God without end.

Discover End

Discover the end of things
And you will have insight into the beginning.
Being last doesn't last always.
Sometimes days are experienced in transition for change.
Days without—
In order to appreciate things received;
Days of mourning and grief—
To appreciate exuberant days of escalating excitement and joy.
Where the Spirit of the Lord is there is freedom[1].
Without—temporary.
Discover the end;
Discover the end
And you will have what you need in preparation.
You will have what you need in guidance and direction.
The end is not all but entails great significance.
Discover the joy of the Lord by seeking His will;
He will not disappoint
Happiness reached through means other than Him
Is but a temporary showing . . .
A light which fades with every flicker.

---

[1] Holy Bible, New International Version®, NIV® Copyright ©1973, 1978, 1984, 2011 by Biblica, Inc.® Used by permission. All rights reserved worldwide. (2 Corinthians 3:17)

Eternal Destiny

Eternally called to fulfill the ways of justice—
Not that one today will make things right,
For that right has already been given
Once by another for all times.
Today's justice is seeing the need and fulfilling it.
Many are called,
Few are chosen.
Few who are called choose to fulfill their destiny,
To focus on one's inadequacies pollutes the mind.
In the process, I am left behind
Without thought for My ability to work through them
That they may fulfill their destiny.
The calling is irrevocable.
The opportunity given.
Another will not come.

Genuineness

All hail the King!
With righteous resolve, we stand and wait by faith
That all will be made well with us.
We favor no other that our hope may be secured in Him.
If not by Him, then who?
The Father of Light.
Our favor, our hope rests in Jesus Christ,
The one who has changed our story from bad to good,
From less to more than enough—
Immeasurable.
We must hold on to our dreams
And let anxiousness subside and fall away
Stand assured, knowing we have what we say
As long as we believe so by faith
And as long as our desires don't give way.
Here it comes,
Riding on a cloud,
Small at first,
But growth is exponential!
What does it mean?
Eyes have not seen, nor ear heard what is prepared for us.
We have His Word;
Therefore, we must trust in Him to fulfill His Word
In mercy and in kindness.
What is our part?
To have patience, assured hope with thanksgiving,
For it was already given when we asked
Nothing less, but more, more, more rings out.
Shout!

The celebration is at hand!
God does not contend with man
But stands to fulfill His Word, complete His Word.
The promises of God are yea and amen
It is done! It is done! It is done!

Heaven's Hill

It's not
The hell on earth that people claim.
One heaven,
One earth,
One hell to be revealed.
The workings of the devil are active until judgment appears;
Heaven is for the faithful alone,
Salvation paves the way for the end.
No Christ, no heaven, no resurrection from the dead—
Is hell the home for the ungodly?
You answer.
How can light and darkness abide together without compromise?
There shall be no compromise!
Hell for the ungodly, the devil, and his angels,
A holding place for judgement.
A new heaven and a new earth shall be established,
A place where righteousness dwells as originally intended.

(Isa 65:17-19; 2 Peter 2:1-9; Rev 21:1-6)

Inner Place

It's from the inner place that I call men
To search for more of Me;
Not by the Word alone;
Not through the pastor or from former messages,
But to truly have a heart which longs for the will of God.
Once the inner place is resolved.
Nothing can deter one from seeking Me in all fullness.
Relationship with Me must be from the place of the heart,
Not for mere knowledge,
Not for material or financial gain.
Not for a spiritual high;
But to honestly and desperately need more of Me.
Search the most inner place of your being
And consider whether the pull is
Too great to exist without the presence of the Lord.
When all is said and done,
The truth of the heart will reveal one's intent,
Whether God is first or not at all.
Things of life grow old with time.
Memories and materials of yesterday fade in midst of today,
And especially tomorrow.
God Almighty and His Word will stand—will last—
For they are eternal.
Should we choose Him, He will be eternally ours
As we are His.
The opposite is also true;
Lies, greed, and deceit will result in temporary gain,
And in the end—
Eternal lost.

Rather than a message of sadness, this is one of hope—
Eternal hope.
Days may seem long and unending but will soon pass,
And only the things done for the glory of God will satisfy
This eternal hope

It's God

Why do we live?
The reason we live?
And if not by Him, how can we live?
Is it in our means to make ourselves who we are?
Or were we already made for a reason,
Created in the image of Him?
Not without a cause He affects us
In hope of a return response from us.
Humanity exists because of Him,
The One, true and only living God.
God gives life;
God gave the breath of life.
Without Him, do we dare exist by our own means?
If so, we must have the meaning of all things;
And if not, then why in part?
Could it be because we partly have meaning of the truth,
And all truth can only be found in Him?
God is before us
If we would recognize His works before us.
There is also work He conveys to us
That He might perform them through us.
Another work—
Kingdom work.
A salvation message.
A work completed on our behalf that we might know Him.
God above all else,
God and no one else.
No other work which must be done
Except that which is already finished.

It's God—
The giver of life and Savior of our soul.
If not by Him, through Him, and for Him,
Then by whom or to what do we attribute the answers of life to?

Innocent Clergy

I have innocent clergy among you—
Those who would give their all for the kingdom of God.
They will stretch themselves far and wide for their faith.
They look to please the Most High
Despite the obstacles of life.
Live a life as such
That you would give all for the kingdom.
In return,
The kingdom will be eternally yours.

Kingdom Come

Thy kingdom come;
Thy will be done.
The Lord's will is to be accomplished through us—
The saved
His glory is manifested in every segment of society,
Every portion of the world.
Our work is to prepare for the second coming of Jesus Christ;
The kingdom of God will come with Him.
There is no shortage of the manifestation of God's glory;
There is no rival to His power;
Nor is there any threat to His throne.
God's will in heaven is to be expressed in the earth.

Knowledge Online

No mercy to the merciless is not the way to be.
You must possess a heart of compassion
Built on a relationship that extends from Me.
The way of the world is not of love, but of hate.
They will hate you even more because you're of a minority fold,
One who's not attracted to the world's attractions.
They will look to sift every piece of evidence of My existence.
With burning ears, they fear the letter of the Word.
With eyes to see, ears to hear, and some pages to unfold,
Allow the story of Christ in you to be told.
The world is not My own
Because it seeks not after Me.
If they were
I would have met them and kept them.
For they are not mine, but you are;
Therefore, you are kept from the disaster to come.
Many are not concerned with the sign of the times.
Humanity will have you believe all is well that ends well,
And live and let live.
If I let them live unto themselves, what would their fate be?
Who has kept with mercy if not I?
The world left to itself will bring destruction to itself
In that it fails to bring to mind the things of God

~ ~ ~

Many consider not the end
Nor do they consider the results of their lifestyle.
I live to bring glory to Me,
And those who fail to see

Or accept Me through My Son,
That lifeline will be cut off as an umbilical cord left untied.

Mercy upon mercy
I rain down acts of love,
But many want to cast it down as something rarely seen.
They fear what people might think.
Thoughts or the mention of My name burns within them
With obsessive hatred.
My kingdom will come.
Let not your knowledge or ways become slack;
Evil will grow in the last days.
Men of darkness will attempt to exploit the men of God;
They will attempt to distort the truth.
Many will believe,
But those who truly know My Word and are guided by My spirit
Will not be shaken or removed.
Know the signs of the time.
Know My Word as never before.
Many will attempt to sift through blatant acts of deception,
But My Word will stand on its own
If you will continuously seek My word on your own,
Then you will have prepared yourself
And not be swept away with the doctrine of demons.

Likewise, My Son

Reveal who the Father is.
The Father and the Son are one.
And the Son has life.
Life through the Son is revealed by our belief in Him.
As Christ fully obeyed the Father
So should believers imitate this behavior toward the Son.
A faithful soul, regardless of the trials of life, and
No matter the outlook.
Our end is secure by faith.
Remain obedient.
Witness the grace which only the Father brings.
The Father is seen in the Son,
For as the Father is, so is the Son.
If we abide in Him
Then the Son should be seen in us.

Mosquito Net

Some are caught in a trap while flowing through life—
An unveiling of sorts
To find one's end as an unsuspected fate.
What waits except an inescapable outcome for the unfaithful.
Have you been faithful?
Then surely rest in the God of all grace.

Origin of Sin

Sin in the beginning;
Sin at the end.
Not so from the beginning, but it began.
At the onset of life
Sin began its deceitful ambition
To undermine and usurp God's authority.
Man's plans, based on sinful intent, only succeed to his destruction.
Sin brought pride along the way.
Selfishness, envy, and murder along the way.
Shame and torment along the way
The way of sin began with words of deceit—
Subtle words offering a form of truth but not in its entirety.
Know the truth,
And you will not be so easily swayed by a lie.
The origin of sin has its beginning,
But it's the end that will confirm the extent of its reality
And dictate the outcome for its deeds.

Puzzle Word

Some words are puzzling, if not completely confusing.
No technicalities needed.
The simple but pure truth of the Word from the Lord suffices.
No other devices.
No works.
And some work a work which dissolves to nothing.
What is done is done.
Accept Him—
The Christ—
By faith in the Word.
Confess the Lord with your mouth
And believe in your heart.
All other works toward righteousness are ritualistic activities,
Suffocating restrictions.
Love and let the Spirit of God work through you
To perform a holy work
Without laws or binding conditions.

~ ~ ~

The Word is not puzzling but simple,
Yet in its simplicity
Are depths of understanding to be searched out.
In searching, you will find
No heart for My Word leaves one puzzled.
No life in Christ only adds to the confusion,
Yet many simple messages abound
Which point to the nature of God.

Revealed wisdom is given to those who search the Word
With intimacy
Whereas those who attempt to feed their intellect
Instead of their hearts
Only receive a portion of the picture painted.

Recognize That

Recognize that you are able to accomplish great things.
Recognize that the challenges often before you
Are not as difficult as they may seem.
Recognize that in Me you can do all things,
And the things you desire most
Become a byproduct
When your obedience starts to sing.

Sheep Breeders

A breeder of sheep
A soft voice speaks
To know a word is to have a word
To say a word
To speak the word of life
Life in someone who is willing to lead and yet follow
To humble themselves
Willing to be used beyond themselves
A leader, a follower
Leading in the way of righteousness
While following the Chief Shepherd

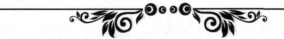

Silent Rage

There will come a time when all will stand still:
The life once lived will no longer matter
If the end does not grant one access to the kingdom.
What will one lose or forsake along the way
For accepting eternally captivity?
Oh, what rage must exist
For those who choose to reject the call of salvation—
Glorious life everlasting—
In exchange for anger in repeated torment!
Not a threat meant to put one to fear;
Instead, an alarm to bring one to reality as God declares.
Many will refuse and some will deny the choice exists.
One end as opposed to another
As if one is not greater and the other much less.
What is even worse
Is that some choose to fully deny
That the days of devastation and torment will exist.
What if you …
What if you miss
A heavenly home in exchange for this?

Silk Screen

Fine linen, fine wear.
What you will wear is a badge of righteousness,
Not of your own accord but of Christ,
For He has caused you to be clothed so.
Many moons will have come and gone
And the one who remains faithful
Shall in likewise fashion be eternally dressed.

Sleep Away

Many of My people sleep away in hope,
But that is as far as some go.
I call for perseverance
That in the midst of difficulties, change may come.
Change is needed where increase is wanted.
Otherwise their latter will be worse than their former.
Many of My people want but sit back and wait
As if they have nothing else to do.
There is work to be done!
Works of righteousness—
Kingdom work,
Working while waiting,
Believing instead of hoping,
And knowing that it is done.

Where thanksgiving abounds, the end is made complete.

Soft Pillow

Pillow top soft.
Some don't want to leave the seat of conformity—
The seat of comfort.
Some settle for less when I have created them for more—
More than they realize.
The focus is within—
Within their own strength and capabilities.
Many fail to see or even entertain the thought
Of what I can do through them.
Pillows are soft—
So soft they lead us to sleep—
Lulling us into a state of lethargy.
Some don't want to wake up, be touched, much less move.
I call for peace, but I also expect work.
The day steadily approaches when all that has been done
Will be tallied for rewards or eternal separation.
Let not sleep or slumber rob you of an inheritance,
Both now and in eternity

Let us work during the day
For the night approaches when no man can work.
(see John 9:4)

Speedway

A compromise of will—
Will the soul be lost or not?
Many travel the fast track of life
Only to settle for Him at the end of life.
What about before then?
Will they come to know Him?
Do you know Him?
If not, take a break from the race
And settle in His place
Of rest.
In it peace,
Joy.
The tempers of life exchanged for the joy in life.
No longer a race to be won
As if it were a race.
A battle to be won, yes—
Of faith.
To endure,
One must learn the ways of righteousness,
And this exists through Christ.
The salvation of the Lord is not to be missed.
For in the end, there will be an account of deeds committed.
Whether bad or good,
Lasting or fading,
A reckoning is coming for all actions,
Reward for the faithful,
An everlasting home through hope in faith.
And for those who wait,
Waiting might result in delaying until it's too late.

Then the fate—
Not to be compared to the life of the faithful,
For in Him alone we live again.
The Christ.

Spared Red

Spared red—
A color in time of difficulty,
A motion set in motion by life.
What is this life?
A way which does not compromise true values.
I value life, but not all men do.
I have repaired the breach which some look to undo.
A brand of red will they receive.
Life for life.
The follies of life follow them.
These destroyers of life seek their own good
While advancing the plan of the enemy.

Have I not left My own in camps hidden?
Dispersed agents of righteousness?
In boldness, they will do the job of many.
They defeat the enemy.
Many are called;
Few are chosen.
Through the few chosen, I will work a work in due season
To win the hearts of men
And save souls condemned to die.

Stored Clues

Clues I leave for My people
For them to gather a notion of My love.
Mine belongs to Me and no other.
How can they detect while others don't?
They look to hear from Me.
They have a desire to know Me.
They seek to fill the void missing
Through Me.
A clue, the word, a sign—
Miracles do not simply happen;
They occur through a presence—
A divine presence—
A hint of reality not seen.

Take In

Taking in but never giving out,
Too many have learned the lesson of slavery—
Slaves to this and that,
Looking to please in order to be pleased,
And never really reaching full pleasure.
Pleasure is found in Me.
Joy inexpressible is found in Me.
As long as I am second fiddle, the search will continue
For happiness, joy, and fulfillment in life.
Many look to draw close to Me
Without knowing Me;
And for those who do know Me,
They must know My will fully.
"Though shall have no other God before Me.²"
I am first or not at all.
Look to please Me.
In doing so,
Your concerns and desires seize my attention.
Too often My people seek this world's pleasure for fulfillment
Rather than learning to trust in Me.
Remain faithful.
I am faithful;
I never disappoint.
By faith, obedience, and with thankfulness receive
The goodness, blessings and promises of the Lord—
I am not negligent concerning My Word.

---

² Exodus 20:3, Deuteronomy 5:7.

Temper, Temper

Learn and discern the temper of the Lord.
He was in a constant state of control
A state of love over emotions
A drive for doing the will of the Father,
As opposed to highlighting the flaws of the people.
Always with the look of love
And a heart which understood the need for change,
In patience,
In guidance,
In needs
He provided.
Though provoked, undisturbed.
Are we required any less or the same?
The same is in us
Because He is in us—
Those who believe

Thy Word

Have you connected to My Word?
Have you abided in My Word so My word can abide in you?
Have you longed to know more of Me?
And has your longing resulted in a greater pursuit of Me,
More understanding,
More commitment,
More devotion,
More awareness,
And more of an outward display of My character?
Search My Word with "all thine heart."
Give Me all,
And I will hold nothing back.
Spend time with Me by spending time in My Word.
With prayer and fasting
Commit to gaining more knowledge, insight, and understanding.
Press toward the high mark of your calling.
In pressing, one must persevere;
In perseverance, remain diligent in seeking Me.

Thy word have I hidden in my heart,
That I might not sin against You.
(Psalm 119:11)

With my soul I have desired You in the night,
Yes, by my spirit within me I will seek You early.
(Isaiah 26:9)

Too Thirsty

Too thirsty for lust
And not enough for Him.
Less of the flesh breeds more zest
For life within Him.
Draw upon the sacrifice paid;
The reward gained;
The end of a matter;
Because the end state is what truly matters.

The Coming of Christ

He is coming!
The Christ!
Have I not set it in My Word?
Have I not spoken it by My prophets?
Christ—
Savior of the world is He,
The One who is to come.
The world waited to see
And saw
But didn't know.
Christ's second coming
Will be for all to see.
The question is will you be ready?

Section 2

SEAMS

All Buts Will Come

We often think the Lord doesn't realize the extent of our problems;
Therefore, we resort to using the word but . . .
But Lord . . .
But you don't know . . .
I know what the Word says, but . . .
We are more than that—
Greater than that.
When we carelessly make excuses, we generate hindrances
To a successful and timely outcome.
Our God moves in the arena of faith.
When excuses and reasoning supersedes faith in times of trials,
We place greater focus on the problem rather than on our God.
Lose the but in order to release the light of day.

Blue and Gray

Shades of light not so light
Shades of blue with gray as a partner.
How much light can be revealed
By uncorking a bottled-up heart?
Light draws dim for some,
But the light of the gospel will dispel the gloom of gray.
The altered colors appear to be at bay
But are unsettled in their minds.

One who wishes to collect on past dues
Bypasses moments of today.
What a perspective!
Far from a full spectrum,
For one ignores the totality of life
In search for the meager things in life.

Carried Away

We are often carried away by the thoughts of the heart,
But the heart, above all things, is deceiving.
We are carried away by the lust of the flesh,
For the flesh is drawn to unrighteousness,
And leads to death.
We are carried away by the thoughts of this world.
This world creates pressure in place of peace.
To be carried away is to lose sight of the way,
For the way adds quality and endurance to life.
In being carried away, some fully lose their way
To the extent of their very soul.

Committed Flare

I hope that all would commit and not run,
To worship and honor in truth
Without doubting.
I have enriched My people,
But many don't understand the ways of faith
Or the extent of their faith
So, they're mostly up and down in faith.
I would that all would remain constant and grow.
This is My heart for My people,
And most of all,
The times dictate it so
Stay in faith without wavering.
Stay in faith and never doubt.
Stay in faith and I will surely show up
To defend you and prosper you.

Farfetched

Farfetched—
A lie, a truth?
Truth seemingly impossible is often considered a lie,
Unless known.
But how are we to know?
Is it within us to know what we need to
Or does the possibility exist, but outside of ourselves?
More is available for the faithful—
Those who believe but have not seen;
Those who are resolved in knowing the truth
And remaining steadfast concerning it,
Despite how farfetched it might seem.

Greater peace, joy, honor, favor and inner strength
Are but a few benefits of a divine relationship.
What is available is only restricted by
Our willingness to believe.

Distinct Reality

A fever-pitched moment,
A fever-pitched night
When the world around us appears vague
As from an indistinct light.
The world around us is seen,
But is everything seen the only reality there is.
Or is there more?
A knowing not known to all,
Not experienced by all.
What men can see; they are willing to believe,
But those who believe without seeing
Are actually the ones who turn the world up-side-down.

If we could see through the eyes of a pioneer or discoverer,
We might then get an idea of picturing things not physically seen.
They were able to see what no one else sees.
They dreamed a different sort of dream.
Their belief and expectation was not of the norm.
Their difference made all the difference,
Uniquely bringing about a change.
They were not reckoned the same.
No one sees what you can see, dream what you dream,
Or are able to envision what you envision.
We are only limited by what we allow ourselves to see.
Our imagination supported by faith
Becomes the instrument where the unbelievable becomes available.

Ideas in Degrees

A degree of ideas.
Many fall short because of no eternal plan,
Only the temporary for vain living—
Living in the prospect of His love without committing in faith
Makes one fall short.
Despite a plethora of ideas being pondered
A commitment to Him is the only valid state.
The salvation of God leads to an eternal inheritance.
And without His salvation, many wait
To see the end of their days
As if the end ends it all.
A day of reckoning is coming because of the fall.
Many have led lives apart from Him.
Many refuse to know or even acknowledge Him.
A commitment persevered because of Him
Leaves no doubt of one's end.
The other is not so worthy,
Not so promising and
Without profit or gain.
To leave the world behind because of Him
Is to have matters settled on your behalf.
To live a full life in Him
Is to be empowered against the dominance of sin.
A gate to be opened,
Another closed.

~ ~ ~

The foretaste of grace given but not recognized;
Instead, flavor of the world erases the hint of grace.
Grace present but unknown
Nor accepted.
Overshadowed by a veil of deception leading to blindness—
Unseeing.
But the truth never fails.
Neither does it fade,
There to keep many from the wicked one
And his dispersed hand.
Rivals, none.
Victory, sure.
If to the end faith is held.

Many Dimes

Many dimes have been dropped, never to be found.
The lost is lost but can be found
If they are found in Me.
Many centuries, much space,
Much time,
And to many places has My love traveled
Only to be rejected.
The time is now to draw nearer to the Lord,
For time waits for no man.
And no man knows what tomorrow holds.
So, suffice it to say, options diminish over time.
Not many days are left for the lost to find a home,
A place of refuge in Me.
Call out to the faithful
That they remain faithful.
Call out to the ungodly
That they might come to know Me.
I am the God who spares, but I am also a just God.
The time draws nearer to the end;
My invitation goes out.
I hope multitudes would respond
When the door is closed, it will be too late,
And those left outside will occupy the place of their appeal.

Many Pieces For

Many pieces for nothing—
Some fall down never to return.
Some fall down in weakness
But are yet strengthen in their return.
The walk of faith consists of many pieces.
Endurance must have its place,
For the walk of faith is a long haul
With many temptations along the way.
Distractions give no limit, for the enemy looks to take our faith
By taking our attention away
From the godly and right thing.
He does so in order divert our focus onto other things
Other than righteous ways.
The life of faith consists of many pieces.
A secured end is preferred over a life without purpose—
Over a life with uncertainty of its end.
And why quit before the end?
We have work to do before then.
We cannot wait for victory;
We must walk in victory.
In the process, lives are being changed.
This is the key to a secured life—
That we not only live in hope of the end,
But that we help secure eternal hope for others
As we live our life of faith.

People End

People often end up saying what they don't want to.
They can't help it because it's in them.
They can't protect themselves by guarding their mouths;
Therefore, they are led in a way unintended.

~ ~ ~

Mercy and peace are found in the mouth;
Power and judgment are found in the mouth.
The extent of one's joy or state of depression
Often originates from one's mouth.
The things we say often lead us
In the direction taken.
Words express the feelings within,
But without,
The cause simultaneously unfolds.
Departing the dock to set sail and achieve things spoken,
The power of the tongue is a mighty thing.
Too often we pay little attention
And forget what we've mentioned
Until it's too late.
People end their careers.
Some allow their marriages to fade from existence,
While others are clinging to life from the words one speaks.
Too often words are spoken without thought,
Destroying years of wonderful experiences.
Focus on your words;
Just as important, focus on the heart.
For out of the mouth is where the abundance of the heart
Is made known.

Playful Pens

Play pens
Place of safety
Place of trust
A place where some enjoy the comfort of home.
A place where others fulfill their lusts.
Driving one to freedom is no freedom at all.
And to live as one supposes freedom is without a relationship
Is truly a life of bondage.
Playing to the crowd or to life's fancies;
Fulfilling the flesh instead of dedicating one's life.
Upside-down is the turn
Unless the life is right with Christ.

Quiet Looms

Quietness looms upon the house of many.
Many do not know
Yet they go
To and fro
As if though
They don't have a care.
Silence never mentions things needed for life.
It cannot show how change can become reality
Unless words are spoken.
And if silent, who benefits whom?
Who is moved, if any at all?
Could it be they have not heard the call
Of salvation ringing?
Call! Call! Call!

Renters Lend

Renters lend
A house of horror.
No longer worthy are the ones who walked away.
No longer worthy are they
When they attempt to rent out their faith,
Talking as if having knowledge
But no longer having a relationship.
The same exists with those who look the part
But are not actually of the fold.

Richmond

Richmond is where contention is.
Many trials exist there.
Many people are not seeing the same thing:
The higher ups versus the lowly desperate—
An image of many cities.
A call goes out for a breach in the lines . . .
For My people to cross the line of separation.
Sustain the fire of desperation
In order to ignite a new fire based on love.
The higher ups are no different.
Terminate the prominence of pride.
Uphold a state of humility.
Battle lines crossed are opportunities
For the love of God to turn an enemy into a friend.

Secrecy, Plans

Many plans are performed in secret—
A needed thing,
Sometimes a meaningful thing.
I have plans of My own.
Plans for you.
Will you search for them by searching for more of Me?
An increased commitment to Me above personal desires
Opens doors designed to release one's destiny
Not only to fulfill one's purpose but to realize one's potential.

Secret Things 2

Secret things,
The down-right nasty things,
Those un-confessed things;
We hate them, but we refuse to let them go.
They challenge with wicked intent our self-esteem and confidence
Yet we keep them closer than a trusted friend.
Some of these things have proven to be detrimental,
Drawing us inward.
As such, we cannot function as we should.
We walk as though an outcast
But only in the circumference of our mind.
These things have done it so,
Keeping us closed up
And we refuse to let them go:
Past hurts,
Uncompleted work,
Abuse set to derail.
And inside it picks away at the character of our being,
Challenging us on the promising and positive,
Discouraging us on many turns,
Keeping us close but never comforting us,
Allowing us to leave up to a point
But never really leaving us.
Inward is the focus while outside is a blur.
It seems to keep one in self-destruct mode,
As opposed to a reliable friend.

I can't believe where I am because of Satan;
He refuses to let me go.
Maybe I should stop pointing the finger,
And maybe it is I who need to deny him so.
These things which keep me bound as if in a straight-jacket:

The hostility,
The rage,
The anger,
The unsettled mind without peace.
And the joy that has been evading me merely creates frustration,
Leading me to pummel the hope of joy in others.
How can I find relief?
How can I be released?
Walls seem to be closing in while these things are picking away.
What can I say?
Or can it be that the answer lies in the things I refuse to say?

These things relish secrecy while despising openness.
Maybe exposure of my inner draining, parasitic foe
Will allow me some relief.
And just maybe I can begin to see clearly,
As opposed to the blur that obstructs my view of reality.
Could it be that my life is not all about me?
At least, in my mind, it is.
Everything not aligned with my order seems out of order.
Can I have control without being controlling?
Can I have love without being demanding?
Can I have peace without putting people's heart in fear?

Can I see change by acknowledging the things within?
Inside is an ugly beast who pretends to have my best interest.
How can I silence his voice and decrease his influence
So I can make decisions not involving him?
Maybe I've said the answer without realizing,
And maybe it's time that I show him
These things I can do without—
Without him, without them.
Freedom springs forth.
Free from self-imprisonment and the raging war within,
Which not only takes its inward toll
But also on those of my close relations.

~ ~ ~

The battle to win lies in freedom of speech—
Free to talk about the inner beast.
Those things that seek our destruction . . .
They have no power.
Only the power which we allow.
A dysfunctional infringement upon a weary soul at best,
Its idea of strength is advancing a twisted reality by deception.

Speak about those things.
Seek forgiveness and repent.
Christ heals all wounds,
Even the picking within.

A divine relationship breaks all ties with wicked attachments

Seams to Love

Love consists of many seams
Following different paths
And made of different colors.
A seamless transition is a conversion from obedience to power,
From the committed faithful
To One found to be trustworthy,
Whom I love enough to let go.
Will you love Me enough to keep it—
To keep Me first
Above all else?
For when all else fails I still remain,
Unchanged.
And still I love.
Let not the seams of life draw you onto an altered path,
A path not meant for you,
A path not for the faithful of heart.

Theatre Proper

What a show; what a show!
The dastardly have delivered so!
We hail the victor of evil intent
While vaguely praising the righteous at heart.
All the excitement given by means of a show—
Entertainment is for all.
But will the wicked steal your heart with violent pleasure
Or will you rest in the pleasures of the Lord?
Movies, see them.
Actors, don't be them.
Influence comes and drives the will.
If not offended,
Then defend Me by your judgment.

Pretenders of righteousness emit a foul odor;
An act worthy of righteous judgement.

Theo Light

God lights the sky,
He enlightens the eyes of the heart
So vision may be attained to reality.
Can there be light without truth?
If truth is given, what is it that blinds the mind's eye?
If not by allowing darkness to take hold
Has the soul been reached or breached?
Breaching brings access for the cause of harm;
Reaching is a way of seeking change
In a manner both pleasing and acceptable to God.
The light of His glory versus darkness which does not give
But only takes, and takes, and takes.
Why lay awake if not for the sake of His glory?
Have you not heard the story
Of Moses's face
Not a sight to behold but revered—
A reverence which brings about fear,
And a fear which binds to love through wisdom.

To Do What I Know

I must do what I know to do,
And if what I'm doing is wrong and I don't know it,
How shall it be made known to me
Unless someone shows me?
Will I give an ear to hear,
Or will I operate in fear,
Totally rejecting without any acceptance of another's belief?
Am I so afraid that I refuse to listen?
What time of day have I given
To interpret the message of the times?
Am I a listener?
A hearer?
Or merely an impulsive rejector
Of everything that ruffles my understanding regarding truth?
The possibility of change exists in attempt for understanding,
But will I allow an air of truth to penetrate
My wall of deflection so change may occur in me?

How we see the word cannot be based on our sole interpretation
And because another believes differently, can it be any less true?
Check with the Spirit of God—
The Spirit of Truth.

There is a Giving-in to "One"

For us or him
The trusted or the foe
Truth and light or darkness and deception
The prevalent does not always win
Though it appears to dominate for a season
A lasting tale is what the journey tells in the end
The righteous right or the defeated foe
One or the other will win

Unknown Region

Unknown regions exist.
Can it be that what's in the abyss
Has caused you to miss
His glory?
Search with truthful intentions of the heart
So truth can be found, and all false agents revealed.
And once found
The vision becomes clear and joy known.
A renewed life lived in truth causes freedom to abound.

Section 3:

PASSION OR PASSIVITY

Bachelor Party

It's all fun and games
Until something attaches itself to you and refuses to let go.
Sin is sensual, soothing, almost hypnotic at times.
A moment of pleasure can destroy a lifetime of promises, purpose,
And commitment to the intended will of God.
More than one night of celebration is the choice of a lifetime—
A refusal of one night's pleasure
For a future that is promising and lasting.

Beauty for Ashes

The beauty of life for the pains of death . . .
What is left of a life without Christ?
The life within is untold by the mind's imagination.
Too much beauty to be expressed by the pen.
The ashes don't cease;
They linger as a stained memory of yesterday's denial,
Opposing the truth of God for the misguided truth of the devil.

(see Isaiah 61:3)

Candid Lid

A lid . . .
A top . . .
A house . . .
How much of love covers all wounds?
Or does love bears all things?
What a trip!
One, who was, forgets who he is.
The one forgiven must not forget
To show the love once shown to him.
Is it not in our strength to strengthen the ones who follow:
And the ones who follow
Must avoid the entrapment of the enslaved.
Take the lid off of love
And display the love of God
So others can be drawn and none forsaken.

Derailed

Set to derail are some,
For they have not given their all to Me . . .
Their heart entirely to Me.
Many have set their course, though I have planned differently.
Derailed,
Though not without hope.
Hope is in Me.
If they would leave the forsaken island of self
And trust in Me,
I will change their course.
Blindfolded are many
Yet they think they can see ahead
Without light
At night.
Current course . . . quite a few travel.
I will shed light if they would come to Me,
Of which some need to return to Me.

(see Isaiah 55:6-7)

Enough

Enough settling and not committing
Enough with living on lies and not in the ways of truth
Enough with not being satisfied
As a result, desperate means are taken
Enough with living on empty
Because all of the ways of God were forsaken

Faith Chapter

Explore the boundaries of faith.
Faith is given in measure
Yet it grows in accordance with our obedience and trust.

~ ~ ~

Have a heart for My Word.
I hold nothing back.
Believers who seek My Word with their whole heart
Will increase faith,
From faith to faith,
A measure of faith to exceedingly great faith.

Floaters

Some come then go,
Some come to stay;
Others lose their way
Because they have not known true commitment.
Such is the way of the Christian walk.
Some are committed,
Some in passing
With highly questionable ambition in mind.
Mine is that all will come to know Me
And serve Me
In spirit and in truth.
Floaters are prone to drifting away.
Hear what I say.
My Word is that you stay
Committed to the Word of God.
Stay committed to relationships.
Stay committed to the calling for which you were called.
There is no other way to see My face
Other than through commitment by faith
To My ways and My will.

Great Faith Challenge

Each believer will be challenged in the arena of faith.
The outcome is often determined by
How much or how little one believes
And whether one believes.
When we can't see it . . .
When we can't see a way out of our trials, do we still believe?
We believe because we take him at His Word.
"He who is in us is greater than he who is in the world."[3]
We face our challenges boldly, with much confidence,
As "He will never leave us or forsake us."[4]
This brings us to another challenge.
Do we take God at his word?
Or do we succumb to blindness, discouragement
And defeat by our challenges?
Accept victory by accepting the Lord God in full assurance.
Our Sovereign God on high

Victory is secure,
But it's our obedience that allows us to cross its threshold.

---

[3] 1 John 4:4.
[4] Deuteronomy 31:6, 8.

Love Unspoken, Yet It Speaks

The unspoken word
Says as much about us as the spoken word.
Action.
This type is love unconditional.
Love My people unconditionally
Then you will know the key to the kingdom.
Love is a universal language which knows no boundaries.
Learn to love in spite of . . .
Regardless of . . .
Love with the love that I have for you,
And you will draw many.
Pull not back, for the day approaches
When speaking to others in the spirit of love-
Will lose its taste for many.
Let not your love for all fall short of My glory.
Love without limits, and you will speak volumes.

Not Long before Night

Night comes quickly to some,
But for all it comes, no doubt.
What does the night season bring if not sleep
Or rest, if you will?
The night comes;
Therefore, it is vital
To accomplish as much work as possible during the day.
When the night comes
Labor ceases,
And a new day will eventually reveal the work completed.

Open Market

The market is full, but where are the workers?
Food for feast is loaded to bear.
But who shall share in its goodness?
My plants are ready to bloom,
But who will replant them
So they may breathe anew and grow?

Oracles

Oracle, oracles.
Writings.
Messages within a message.
The message of God is for the faithful,
To draw the unsaved,
To encourage those wavering in faith,
To build up the body of believers.

~ ~ ~

I have written, so let it be.
No adding, no taking.
Simply trusting Me at My Word.
My Word does not harm;
It increases faith and the stature of believers who search for Me
In truth.

Parameters of Faith

Faith justified is faith seen
Not the faith that is clearly visible,
Rather that which is seen in obedience to the things heard.
Evidence of faith is what I am after.
No one can tell you, you don't have faith,
But you can tell them by your actions.

Passionate Release

Passion upon My people
I have kept to this day.
Will they not seek the way to salvation?
For it is at hand.
True believers are to work a work in due season—
In all seasons—
For the harvest is ready, but the laborers are few.
I have passion for everyone,
But will everyone receive the message of the gospel?
Surely not.
This doesn't mean My people should try any less
In seeking their salvation.
Live out My passion for reaching lost souls
So they may find life in Me.
The passion released is passion restored to overflow,
For then you are walking in My will;
And in My will is where all needs are met.
Desires become a reality
And lack is prevented entry.

Passively Waiting

Dare we think that we can passively wait, doing nothing,
And enter into the glory of the Lord?
As an heir,
Do we dare not accept the bruises laid on by the plow at work?
Are we resolved to alienating ourselves
To the comfort of the church walls
While others walk in danger, being preyed on to death?
Where is your spiritual health?
Should you not be disturbed by those who are victimized
And allow believers' victimization
To push you to a point of participation?
Employing gifts, utilizing resources, and fulfilling one's calling—
These commit to
As being a blessing in the midst of offering a sacrifice.

Preach Well

Preach well, preacher,
For the time will come
When many will not endure sound teaching.
Preach well
And don't forsake your calling through weariness.
Preach well,
For in doing so
A light is given, though not always received.
Preach well, for this is your calling.
Preach well
Whether others receive it or not,
For this is what you were called to do.

Rolls Away

Sin rolls away from some—if not many—
For those who know how to seek forgiveness.
Others lounge in unforgiveness.
They become engulfed by it;
Therefore, they continue to seek its vain pleasures,
As opposed to seeking forgiveness and true repentance.
Many are the fallen,
But the favor of the righteous shall stand.

Rewards of Our faith

The reward of our faith is satisfaction in knowing
God is in control.
Our works do not apply to His goodness,
Rather in our favor apart from salvation.

Sit This One

Can we really afford to sit this one out?
Do we have time to take time off
From the call of salvation?
How many ways and how many days
Are there to commit to?
And when the time comes who do we turn to?
Do we finish when we're finished
Or do we stop between now and then?
A vacation is not the same as stepping away
Or putting off today
Words needing to be said pertaining to life.
Don't sit this one out.
Instead, stand in the gap.
Who knows when or how the time will come
Or be lost
If we allow ourselves to vacate our responsibility?

Steamboat

Steamboat
Running down the line at one time
Not so much today
For it has made way for new
Cruise line cruising
Bringing entertainment
Amusing
No defeat
No retreat
But forcefully advancing if you will

~ ~ ~

Will mine spend the time
With Me
In My Word
In prayer
For in Me is favor
But many do not favor Me
Still
Spread My Word
Speak My Word
Though seasons and time changes
My Word never changes
I left My Word for men to seek after Me
To learn from Me
For everything spoken isn't spoken by Me
My Word is the key
For My Word brings you continually close to Me
As opposed to you being one
Who has faded into a distant memory

The Challenge of Staying Close

We often lose sight of the important things
In exchange for minor things that we deem important:
The love of our life,
The giver of life,
The lives we created.
The challenge of staying close
Is knowing when to say enough is enough
Against the outer distractions.
Staying focused means not losing sight of those most dear.
Soothing, insignificant,
Sometimes boldly daring enticements will come,
But it is for us to keep our focus on Him,
Our God.
Whether man or woman, we have been completed in love,
And we are to foster the importance of a divine relationship
In loved ones who the Lord has given us from above.

Section 4:

LIFE LESSONS

(THE LIGHT OF KNOWLEDGE)

Annual Duty

A yearly duty to some,
But every day is expected.
To live for the glory of the Lord
Self becomes second, that life in Him will take hold.

Let Go

Let go of all that is
For He who is all

Nothing Less

Nothing less than a grave sacrifice will do—
One dying to oneself
That life may be found anew

The Skinny

Information content
Too often time is spent in searching to know more,
But not enough is spent in searching to know more of Me.
Many search for information instead of a relationship.
Information will get you some knowledge,
But is there a sincere desire to be closer to Me?

Revelation is based on the heart
With a deep desire for Me as well as My word.

Beyond the Cutting Board

Beyond the cutting board, there's a stake—
An object designed to point to a place,
Setting boundaries or securing a direction.
What difference does this make?
Without the guide, ways become difficult, if known at all.
A cutting board to prepare,
A stake to guide,
A friendship in an odd relationship,
Yet it's a formidable pair used to destroy one's pride.
Arrogance has deception in it, needing to be stamped out.
Unless revealed, one will follow the path of error.
The stake brings direction.
If unknown, then the way cannot be known.
The stake guides the way
The cutting board corrects and prepares one for the way.

College Harms

College harms no one.
Institutions are set up for increased learning
And prepares the minds and heightens a sense of destiny—
An inspiring taste to add to greater humanity.
Children need school, though some might disagree.
It is as avenue of preparation and change,
An enlightenment in universal advancement.
It gives insight into what could be.
Discover a role
And you will find that learning gives the edge.
Don't fear school;
Instead use it as a tool
For greater opportunities in life.
Welcome it.
Embrace it—
The opportunity to receive more
In order to be better equipped
To do more.

Desolate Being

Some barren.
Some blessed.
Some live without hope
While others live to confess
The hope they have found:
There is none but one who saves,
That is, if you believe He saves.
The desolate man sees no hope.
We must show them hope
In Christ.
The desolate man worries.
The only fear we should have is of God.
This brings wisdom and understanding,
As opposed to intimidation or trepidation.
Desolate men are often disheartened.
Brokenness is where the Lord begins;
He draws near to a broken and contrite heart
Desolation is but a moment in time,
And more importantly,
Is the time we should take in getting to know Him—
The Christ.

(Inspired by: Ps 138:6, 7: Ps 34; Ps 103:11, 17;
Ps 111:10-112:1-3; Ps 115:13-14; Ps 145:17-20)

Filled but not Satisfied

Forsake the bad girls,
For they cloud judgment by way of the flesh.
Forsake the strong men,
For with enticing words they play a game
Only to leave you in distress.
Forsake selfish glory,
For this work does a death.
Will you forsake all for Me
And receive fulfillment to depths unimaginable?

Frost Grain

The coldness of the night
Light lit low for some
To appease the taste of a sensual mood.
A grain of food.
How can a little morsel satisfy
When a feast is readily available?
That which seems tasty
Is often lined with hazards meant to destroy.
A grain frozen is immobilized
Light is brought for the dealing of things—
Hidden things.
A revealing if you will for what is done in darkness.
By light most pay the bill
A grain for a day
Or a feast for a lifetime

Mint

Mint
As green as envy.
Do we die?
Do we lie
Or do we rely on what we've come to know?
Some tickle the fancy only as a distraction against the Word.
Some hear but relish in only what others have come to know.
To know My Word is to know Me.
To seek another's gift
Is a portion of the sinner's heart indicating greed.

Rage's Lid

There is no lid for the righteous
Rages of honor, no honor
Rages in life, no life
Mercy shown in the midst of compassion steals the show
Rage puts a lid on love
It is not bound by it
Instead it binds the ability to love
To love in spite of all the turmoil above
That of the mind
And the damaging fragments left behind

Thirsty Land

The land is parched;
Furthermore, getting dryer.
Where barrenness exists, dysfunction sets in.

X Rated Love

We love to ride the emotion of an adulterous scene.
We quiver with anticipation for what might be,
But surely this is all a setup.
Gravitation to the flesh, if you will,
To appease the flesh more than abiding in holiness.
This too is a gift—
That you remain holy,
That you be holy
Even as I Am.

Section 5

LIFE

Children's Bread

Healing for a nation
. . . For us . . .
Was performed on our behalf.
We simply need to accept it,
Receive it.
Many don't believe
And their condition remains the same.
Faith cometh by hearing and hearing by the Word.[5]
Increase your faith,
And you will increase your ability to receive
That which is already given.
Faith lacks no tolerance, but believes
In spite of the report given . . .
In spite of circumstances and situations
Which appear in opposition of My Word.
It is done by faith.
It is made complete and whole by faith.
That which you desire is made possible...
Only by faith.

Acknowledge the history of My works,
And you will refuse to settle for any negative report.

---

[5] Romans 10:17.

Confessions of a Blind Man

Some speak.
Who will listen?
If all speak, will any listen?
To be heard is to have a voice.
To say much;
To say little:
What choice is there and whose choice is it?
On whether one is heard or not:
Can we see?
Can we tell?
With a quick judgment, not so.
But then again, with the blind maybe so.
The blind have eyes to see,
But they are that of the mind.
What the mind sees is heard by the ears
Giving sight to the unseen when heard.
What men don't see, will they be able to conceive in their mind?
Let's look at Abraham—
Having no knowledge of multitudes,
He saw the starry night being led by God.
He received vision, though, at first, he did not understand,
So are they who don't know Him—
The Christ—
They are blind of sight.
No vision is given because of rejection
And only possessing
A limited degree of truth.

Dietary Rights

Rights to life
Not found in food
But bread will do for a day
If you make your days complete
With His daily bread

(Based on Matthew 4:4)

Distinct Life

A life of gold, even silver.
A life without regrets.
A full life without limits.
Regardless of what's seen or felt,
Life revolves around knowing in one's heart
That what he believes is true,
That everything and more than one desires
Is found in a life that is lived in truth.

Forfeiture of Life

Often is the case where many forfeit life.
Many people live to please themselves
As if pleasure in life is life's greatest reward.
One of the greatest rewards is having received life from another.
How can we begin to focus outward
When our focus is mainly on ourselves?
The less we see, the more we are able to do,
And the more we see, the more we want.
In the process, many things are being missed.
This for that . . .
We give up things in order to have things,
But many times, the things given up
Are costlier than the ones attained.
Refrain your lips from speaking evil;
Refrain your tongue from cursing and curses.
A move toward God is a step in the right direction.
To complete the path by faith is the greatest reward of them all!

Generic Life

A life of hope without belief
Seeing things hoped for is really not belief at all;
Belief is believing in that which is not seen
Yet held true in the mind of the believer.
A generic life is a life of vague understanding,
Very little commitment,
And tyranny against the faithful.
Those who believe must hold true
The spoken Word,
The written Word.
Vagueness incorporates doubt.
Mildly committing leads to wondering;
And wondering leans toward defection.
I have hope for them,
But they fail to see the grace given.
I plead for them,
Yet they turn their backs at every hint of trouble.
I send for them,
Yet when knocking, I receive no answer.
A backward people led by backward deeds
With the only consolation being small-minded appreciation.
If you appreciate Me then serve Me fully.
If you love Me
Then refuse to turn your back on Me as with a jilted lover.
Exposed truth is an opportunity for Me to draw close.
Will you accept the truth totally,
Or will you deny it?
In doing so, you chose your type of relationship with Me.

Heritage Ends 2

Heritage ends for those without life—
Life in the Son is life eternal,
If life perseveres until the end.
Promote life with the tongue.
The living among the dead . . .
The living out of dead things.
The past is not your future,
But your future can be spoken into life by your words.
Bring life that you may live and not die,
Thereby, putting an end to dead things.

Lost Life

A lost life is a grave sacrifice
For it returns not
But gives Sheol its due
The price paid for salvation denied

~ ~ ~

Some unselfishness in the walk of righteousness
Leads the way to the saving of a soul
Selflessly give
In this, others can live
Self dies that in the end, souls are gain

Marble

Marble falls.
What falls except My Word upon the heart of the faithful,
The hungry, and the unsettled?
My Word falls upon the hearts and minds
Of those who desire Me more than life itself.
To love Me is to seek Me;
To seek Me is to find Me;
To find Me is to find life
And all the riches of My kingdom in glory.
There is no lack for the faithful, as some might consider lack.
Every need is supplied, though some may tarry.
A gift is given to all—
Salvation,
The promise of the Spirit,
Life eternal for the steadfast.
Rewards are given but only received in the end.
What will you have seen and endured between now and then?
Salvation calls,
But the end will tell of one's faithfulness.

Natural Life

It's natural for some to lie
Their father taught them so
Sin seated in the beginning still holds its place today
Many have felt the sting of its effects, though painless
Unless
It is pain associated with the end of all things

Puzzle Me

Puzzle me about life and I quiver.
Teach me what it means to live;
Then you will have planted seed for a fruitful end.
Be not puzzled about the qualms of life.
Life with strife is a part of life.
No strife, no growth.
No testing, no development of character.
What then
If not the end being met with hardship?
Having nothing from the front
Leaves a slim chance of standing when all is said and done.

Origin of Life

The origin of life.
What is life?
Is it all that we know
Or is there more to know?
Life, in itself, is inexpressible and far too complex
To be articulated by the limited vocabulary of men.
A portion of life is understood in knowing the Father,
Yet all of life is too much to comprehend.
What then?
Should we search for understanding as best we can,
Or are we resolved in knowing as little as possible
And allow life to have its way?
There is a way to life which seems right to men.
Then there is the truth about life
Which only comes through a relationship with the Creator.
Look to know God personally,
Intimately.
Then you will begin to know about life.
Life apart from God is really no life at all.
Life apart from God has temporary pleasures as its goal.
Life in Christ breeds life eternal,
For there is life after this
If we truly believe that He exists.
For those who don't
The life they see may be the only life they will see.

Original Sin

Original sin
The separation of man from God.
What made his return possible
If not by the precious blood of Christ?
In our separation, we forfeited eternal life.
In our separation, we gave up our authority.
In our separation, we condemned ourselves
And brought ourselves beneath God's original intent.
No longer is this the case—
The wall of separation has been broken by Christ,
Giving us access to the Father.
The separation, once a reality, is now taken away.
The guilt from sin no longer has its condemning effects.
Instead we are redeemed!
For good works of righteousness,
To hold sway concerning that which gives eternal life.
No longer does sin have its dominating persuasion,
For the guilty have been made righteous,
And the righteous, priests and kings!

Priests shine the light of God's glory
As king's authority is given to rule as God first intended.

(Inspired by 1 Peter 2:9; Rev 1:5-6; Matt 5:14,16; Phil 2:15)

Pointless Edge

What is the point?
Moreover, where is the point
Which brings sharp contrast to what is considered normal?
A normal seductively being changed by the evil of night,
Now the abhorrent, appears as if right.
Have we lost our sight?
Have we drifted away from the edge—
The edge of life,
The edge of ourselves?
Have we become more accustomed to society's norm—
A norm descending into a new stage in life—
A life away from God,
A life with a frightful end?
Though many will say, "It's not that bad,"
Are we not living on the edge,
Knowing that eternity is but a step away?
And if that close,
Should we not be more careful and purposeful in our living?
Should we not be more impromptu in our giving?

~ ~ ~

The edge of sanity . . .
The center of reason . . .
Will we live as if the end is near
Instead of trying to avoid the inevitable
For the temporary days of summer?
It will change at some point—
Life.

It will come an end—
The edge.
And the things we do between now and then
Will account for what we leave behind.
And more importantly,
The rewards that await us on the other side of life's doorway.

Presence, the Life

Most squander it;
Some never live it;
Others are afraid of it
While never really embracing it.
Why pass this way without a way of remembering?
It is not for us but for those who follow.
Should our lives not echo things from the past
That are needed for today
As our children take on their tomorrows?
If not for us, then for them
Embrace life
And let life be found in Him,
The Christ.
So our children can be prepared for tomorrow.
So our ways can affect the direction taken.
It's not about us, instead about Him,
But we also do it for them.

Our actions through salvation help determine generational blessings.
Of this, we have a responsibility.

Reference Code

A code to be tested and built—
Built upon a foundation.
Not this for that
But Him for his,
For He fails not.
A code speaks of freedom,
Release,
Access to the hidden.
Many do not know the way of life.
Instead, they filter the matters of life within their minds,
Concluding they know the way without knowing Him.
How could this be?
Have they not learned
The fear of God is the key
To understanding the way of life?
This is the secret to knowledge and wisdom:
By fearing Him, we begin to see how life unfolds
And where it ends,
And between the two
Why things happen, though not all is explained.
Know Him to know life.
Without, we are barely scratching the surface of life
With no way of accessing the truth of life
As it really exists.

Society's Clues

Society has a clue but really no solid idea—
A vague understanding, if you will—
Concerning who believers know and believe.
He who exists but is not seen
We believe because we know Him.
Furthermore, we take Him at His Word,
For His Word reveals life
And the greater mysteries of life.
Oh! The clue from a different order is in order!
One who knows
Can introduce the One who is known
To those who might believe.
It is for them to receive
After having heard.
And in hearing, the clue is given
That it might forge an understanding
Through a committed relationship.

Days of thunder lie low.
Too many diseases have caused many not to believe so
That life and greater life exists among the living,
Though appearing different by means of the time.

Sophisticated Facet

There is a sophisticated life
Which does not close with a favorable end.
Then there is the end with joy everlasting.
The sophisticated life has many facets.
Not all, but many, end without triumph.
The little things spoil the vine.
Though wealth is not a bad thing,
Sophistication tends to balance itself on pride,
And pride leads to death—
A fall.
A sense of dignity without digging a grave,
For the grave takes no hold
Of one who has the Redeemer as Lord.
A life of sophistication is a life not well spent,
But great is the one who balances this life
In expectation of the One to come.

Sprout Life

Life sprouts for all,
But what is the extent of one's life from birth?
Some live long but remain dead along the way.
Others have forsaken their way
That they may gain life through death.
Victory is sure for the faithful—
For those who remain faithful until the end.
What then
Of those who live wickedly in this present world?
Yours is to intercede on their behalf;
Reach out with My Word
As not to allow your salvation to be in vain,
But rather lived out in righteousness,
Being obedient to the Word.

Stakeout

Stakeout the life of the living.
Have all lived for Me and died to Me?
It's not so.
If not for Me then for whom?
Everyone lives for something or someone
And dies to someone or something.
Life is more than merely living,
Rather to be lived for the One who lives.
Wonder why people cry who have no hope?
Wonder why people are sad as if the end ends it all?
We have but to call
So they may live.

~ ~ ~

There is life in Me.
There is eternal resting favor in Me.
Many are sad about the end because they don't know the end,
But the end does not have to end without Me.
Stakeout life and see how people move to and fro
With so much busyness as if making headway.
Unknown to them,
They are caught in a life-size Ferris wheel
Revolving in circles
With an unsuspected end.

Life is worth living for the hopeful.
Give them hope through My Word,
For it is eternal.
So is life in Me.

Struggle Life

Life is not all about struggles
Oftentimes there is a need for pressing
In pressing one is being strengthen
No struggle, no strife
How can one be victorious unless there is a fight
A fight for one's faith
Not that it is unsettled
For in Me it is

Sustain Life

Sustaining life
From His breath to our hearts,
That we may grow in grace of His Word.
Let His Word be heard so we can save some.
How shall our lives be sustained if not by Him,
The Savior of men,
Who was, is, and is to come?
Until then,
Let His work be done.

Warrior Life

The life of a warrior—
A fight, for it's always on.
Victory gained by strength of faith.
A desire to wait increases the possibility of captivity
Brought on by a spirit set to derail.
Hail! Hail! Hail!
The King speaks!
One who wishes to endure must not settle in defeat,
But rather defend.
Defend his faith he must!

Whole Life

The whole of life
In its entirety . . .
What is left of life once we have left?
Does it merely move on without our existence?
If so, which appears so,
Will we have added to or detracted from life?
Ours is to build up and promote life,
As opposed to sanctioning death.
Ours is to live and enhance the quality of life
For others as well as ourselves.
What is left to tell after we leave?
Will the things we've done be spoken of admirably
Or will they be forgotten as an indistinct memory?

Windows of Eternity

Let loose the stars
For I have set them free!
Raise the eye to the heavenly constellation,
For I alone created them
A bliss not to be missed but to reflect upon.
Can you see?
Can you see beyond the stars into eternity?
Let not your vision be blinded by lack of light
Or dimmed from darkness.
Realize there is more than meets the eye.
Look into the sky.
If you see them you see Me.

A book for now
As if now was then
That time to come
Before it comes
The call
Salvation!
For the Kingdom of God is at hand!

A pleasure, a delight
His message of mercy
The Father of Light
Shedding light
On the need for faith and the kingdom to come
His kingdom on earth

The kingdom is and yet to come
The prepared welcome such an event
The unlearned are scarcely aware
A day of reckoning in the making
Days of mercy before then
Who will abide
Who will stay true
A message of deliverance before judgement
And surely the Lord will have His day

Printed in the United States
By Bookmasters